Thomas Hodgins

The Canadian Franchise Act, 1885

Thomas Hodgins

The Canadian Franchise Act, 1885

ISBN/EAN: 9783337205102

Printed in Europe, USA, Canada, Australia, Japan

Cover: Foto ©Suzi / pixelio.de

More available books at **www.hansebooks.com**

SUPPLEMENT

TO THE

CANADIAN FRANCHISE ACT, 1885,

CONTAINING

THE AMENDING ACT OF 1886

(49 *VICTORIA, CHAPTER* 3).

WITH EXPLANATORY NOTES

BY

THOMAS HODGINS, M.A.,

ONE OF HER MAJESTY'S COUNSEL, AND EDITOR OF "HODGINS' ELECTION CASES,"
"MANUAL ON VOTERS' LISTS," ETC.

TORONTO:
ROWSELL & HUTCHISON, LAW PUBLISHERS.

1886

ROWSELL AND HUTCHISON, PRINTERS TORONTO.

INDEX OF CASES.

TABLE OF THE ELECTORAL FRANCHISE.

Title of Voter.	Occupation of Premises, or Residence in the Electoral District.	Value.
Real Property Franchise.		
(1) *Owner—* (a) in his own right.. (b) in right of wife .. (c) his wife owner ..	Ownership prior to or at the date of the revision of the Voters' Lists	Cities, $300. Towns, $200. Other places, $150.
(2) *Occupant—* (a) in his own right.. (b) in right of wife . (c) his wife occupant.		
(3) *Farmer's Son—* (a) Father owner.... (b) Mother owner ..	Both occupation and residence for one year next before : (1) the date of his being placed upon the List of Voters ; or (2) the date of the application for the placing of his name on the List of Voters	Farm, or other real property, if equally divided among the father and sons, or (if mother the owner) among the sons, sufficient, according to the above values, to give each a vote.
(4) *Owner's Son—* (a) Father owner.... (b) Mother owner ..		
(5) *Tenant*		$2 monthly, or $6 quarterly, or $12 half yearly, or $20 yearly.
(6) *Tenant-farmer's Son—* (a) Father tenant .. (b) Mother tenant ..		
(7) *Fisherman* (owner)..	Prior to or at the date of the revision of the Voters' Lists	$150, land, boats, fishing tackle, &c.
(8) *Indian*		$150 of improvements.
Income Franchise.		
(9) *Income*	Prior to or at the date of the revision of the Voters' Lists, and one year's residence in Canada ..	$300 a year.
(10) *Annuitant*.........	Residence for one year prior to the revision of the Voters' Lists......	$100 a year.

SUPPLEMENT

TO THE

CANADIAN FRANCHISE ACT.

49 VICTORIA, CHAP. 3.
Canada.

An Act to amend the Act respecting the Electoral Franchise and the Dominion Elections Act, 1874. (*a.*)

[*Assented to 2nd June, 1886.*]

WHEREAS it is expedient to amend " *The Electoral* reambl. *Franchise Act,*" (*b*) and " *The Dominion Elections*

(*a*) Where the amendments consist of words added to the clause of the original Act, they are indicated by square brackets []; and where certain words in the original Act are struck out, references are made to the alterations in the notes.

(*b*) Several of the amendments made by this amending Act to the original Act remedy defects, or ambiguities, pointed out in the Editor's notes to the *Canadian Franchise Act of 1885.* But some of the new clauses appear to create other ambiguities which may require further legislation, and which will be found more fully referred to in the notes. It has been well said by an eminent legal writer : "A Bill usually goes into Parliament in the state in which it ought to come out ; and comes out in the state in which it ought to go in. An ordinary statute differs from an ordinary deed much as a marriage settlement, prepared by a competent lawyer, differs from one which should be finally settled in a dozen fierce wrangles between the heated relatives of the happy pair. If testators, when making their wills, were to put in new clauses on the spur of the moment ; or the respective families were to cut out the drafts of an eminent conveyancer, wills and settlements would have

Act, 1874," (c) as hereinafter set forth : Therefore Her Majesty, by and with the advice and consent of the Senate and House of Commons of Canada, declares and enacts as follows :—

S. 2 of 43-49 V., c. 40, amended.

1. Section two of the Act first cited is hereby amended by striking out the definitions of "owner" (when it relates to the ownership of real property situate elsewhere in Canada than in the Province of Quebec) "occupant," "father," "mother," "farmer's son," "son of an owner of real property," and "actual value" or "value," (d) and inserting the following in lieu thereof :—

"Owner" elsewhere than in Quebec.

"The expression 'owner,' when it relates to the ownership of real property situate elsewhere in Canada than in the Province of Quebec, means the proprietor either in his own right, or for his own benefit, or if such proprietor is a married man it means proprietor in his own right, or in the right of his wife, [or the person whose wife is such proprietor (e)] of freehold estate, legal

---

a strong resemblance to modern Acts of Parliament :" *2 Law Quarterly Review 133.*

(c) The only amendment which this Act makes to the Dominion Elections Act, 1874, is in respect to the forms of oaths to be taken by voters at elections. The Act of 1874 (ss. 43 and 44 amended by 41 Vic. c. 6 s. 5), provided that the oath or oaths of qualification to be taken by a voter at an election for the Provincial Legislature, should be applicable to elections to the House of Commons—the words : "House of Commons of Canada" being substituted therein for the words : "House of Assembly," in such oath or oaths.

(d) The striking out of the above definitions affects some of the notes on pp. 22, 37, 45 and 48 of the original work.

(e) "The person whose wife is such proprietor." This amendment settles the question discussed in the notes on pp. 22-29, 40 and 75 of the original work, viz. : the right of a husband to qualify and vote in respect of his wife's property in those Provinces where recent Provincial Legislation had altered the

or equitable, (*f*) in lands and tenements held in free and
common soccage, of which such person [or the wife of Where wife owner.
such person] is in actual possession, or in respect of
of which such person [or the wife of such person] is in

---

common law, and had divested the husband of the freehold interest formerly
acquired by marriage in his wife's real estate. But in the Provinces
where the common law has not been altered, the term "proprietor in right
of his wife," recognizes the husband's scisin in feo in his wife's real estate, by
virtue of the marriage. The effect of the above amendment is to make the
husband of a married woman her representative for the purpose of the franchise, and to give legislative sanction to a new principle in Parliamentary .
elections, namely, that the representative of an owner of real property may
vote at elections, for or as the delegate of such owner. The same point was
referred to in the latter part of note (*e*) p. 79 of the original work, in com-
menting on the case of persons who, having no estate in the qualifying property, but only a relationship to the owner of such property were invested
with a statutory franchise. It may also be contended that the wife having the
ownership of the property becomes entitled to that which is incident thereto,
viz., the right to the franchise ; and that the husband, who has no estate or
interest in her property, exercises, by virtue of his marriage, such political
right as her agent, and marks the ballot for her. The above amendment
may be said to recognize this principle of representation, or "voting by
proxy," at elections; and it apparently sanctions in respect to married women,
what appears to have been the ancient practice of unmarried women—of voting
by attorney at Parliamentary elections : "Whether women have not anciently
voted for members of Parliament, either by themselves or attorney, is a great
doubt. I do not know upon inquiry, but it might be found that they have :"
Per Lee, C. J., in *Olive v. Ingram*, 7 Mod. 269.

(*f*) Where an association of persons had purchased land for a Stock
Exchange, and vested it by deed in trustees upon such terms that the
individual members of the association were respectively entitled only to a
share in the net profits of the Exchange : *Held*, that such persons had not
an equitable freehold in the land, only an interest in the profits of the concern, and, therefore, no right to vote, although the association was not
incorporated, but was a mere voluntary organization without statutory
powers or restrictions : *Watson v. Black*, 16 Q. B. D. 270. See further
notes (*l*) to (*t*) pp. 22-34, of the original work.

receipt of the rents and profits ; (*g*)

"Occupant."   "The expression 'occupant' (*h*) means a person in actual occupation of real property otherwise than as 'owner,' 'tenant,' or 'usufructuary,' in his own right, or in the case of a married man in his own right or in the right of his wife, [or whose wife is in such actual occupation,] and who [or whose wife] receives to his [or her] own use and benefit the revenues and profits thereof; (*i*)

"Father."
"Mother."   "The expression 'father' includes grandfather, step-father and father-in-law; and the expression 'mother' includes [grandmother,] (*j*) stepmother and mother-in-law;

"Farmer's son."   "The expression, 'farmer's son, means [and includes the son of an owner and actual occupant of a farm or of a tenant and actual occupant (*k*)

(*g*) See as to the husband's right of possession and of occupation of his wife's property note (*a*) p. 40 of the original work.

(*h*) See notes (*x*) to (*b*), pp. 37-40 of the original work.

(*i*) See note (*x*) p. 75 of the original work.

(*j*) The only change made by this amendment is the addition of the word "grandmother," referred to in note (*k*), p. 80 of the original work as not included in the definition of "mother."

(*k*) This amendment partially remedies a defect referred to on pp. 45 and 54 of the Editor's notes to the original Act, extending the right to vote to the sons of "tenants" who are "actual occupants of farms under a lease of not less than five years." The original clause read: "Farmer's son means any male person not otherwise qualified to vote, and being the son of an owner and actual occupant of a farm." The amendment repeats the words "owner and actual occupant" commented upon in notes (*j*) and (*l*), p. 45 of the original work; and in construing the words "tenant and actual occupant of a farm" the same observations may be applicable. The extension of the franchise to the sons of tenants of farms, appears, from the proceedings in the House, to have been made during the final stages of the Bill, and apparently without attention having been called to the necessity of some amendments to

of a farm (*l*) under a lease for a term of not less than
five years;]

"The expression 'son' (*m*) includes a grandson, step- "Son."
son and son-in-law ;

"The expression 'actual value' or 'value' means the "Actual value," or
then present market value of any real property, if sold "value."
upon the ordinary terms of sale (*n*) : Provided, that the
assessment rolls, as finally revised for municipal purposes,
shall be *prima facie* evidence of the value of such property."

---

sub-s. 7 (*b*) of the substituted s. 3 *post*, so as to adapt that sub-sec. to the
case of tenant-farmers' sons resident on the farm with their *mother*, after the
death of the father. See note (*m*) to that sub-s. p. 17 *post*. Independently of
the doubt whether the franchise has been extended to the sons of a tenant of
a farm, where the mother is tenant after the death of the father, the above
amendment does not go to the full extent referred to in notes (*j*) p. 45, or
(*z*) p. 54, of the original work. The following "farmers' sons" appear to be
still excluded from the franchise :

(1.) Sons of tenants of farms—
    (*a*) Where the lease is for less than five years ;
    (*b*) Where such lease is for a term of five years, but is not in writing.
        See note (*l*) p. 69, of the original work.
(2) Sons of occupants of farms.

(*l*) The definition of "farm" remains as before : *i. e.*, " land *actually occupied by the owner thereof*, and not less in quantity than twenty acres."

(*m*) The words struck out of the original Act are the two definitions of
"farmer's son" and "son of an owner of real property," and the substitution
of the above. See notes (*j*) to (*m*) pp. 45, 46, of the original work.

(*n*) The amendment made to this definition in the original Act is by
striking out from this part of the clause the words : "in respect of which any
person claims to be qualified whether as owner, tenant, occupant, or farmer's
son, or other owner's son, as determined by the Revising Officer upon the best
information in his possession at the time of such revision." The effect of
this amendment of the original clause, and of s. 10 *post*, amending s. 33 of

2

Ss. 3 and 4 repealed; new provision.

2. Sections three and four of the said Act are hereby repealed, and the following substituted therefor (o):

Who shall be registered as voters if qualified as to—

" 3. Every person shall be entitled to be registered in any year upon the list of voters for the proper polling district of any electoral district or portion of an electoral district, and when so registered to vote, if such person—

Age.

" (1.) Is of the full age of twenty-one years, (p) and is

Not disqualified.

not by this Act or by any law of the Dominion of Canada disqualified or prevented from voting ; (q) and

---

the original Act, is to exclude from the consideration of the Revising Officer in preparing the preliminary lists of voters, any other evidence of the value of the voter's real property than that furnished by the assessment roll, leaving it to those who dispute the correctness of the valuation in the roll to give such evidence as will displace the *prima facie* affirmative which the law imputes to the Assessment Roll. See notes on pp. 48-50 of the original work ; and also the note (v) p. 50 as to *prima facie* evidence.

(o) The substitution of this section for sections 3 and 4 of the original Act consolidates the two sections into one, and settles some ambiguities which had been pointed out in notes (n) p. 70, (e) p. 71, (r) p. 72, (x) p. 75, (h) and (l) p. 80, of the original Act. Sub-s. 10 of this section adds a new class of voters to the electorate, after the year 1886.

(p) See notes (a) to (d) pp. 54-59, of the original work.

(q) A person having an *inherent legal incapacity* to be an elector, should be struck off the voter's list after notice ; and in case the notice of objection is defective, all necessary amendments of such notice should be allowed under s. 43 of the original Act. See note (a) p. 156, and note (m) p. 137. The Judge should amend the notice so as to accord with the true state of facts : *Per* Moss, C. J., *Opinions on the Voters' Lists Acts*, Case No. 6, p. 10. " If persons have no right to vote, they can have no right to be on the register :" *Per* Byles, J., in *Earl Beauchamp* v. *Madresfield*, L. R. 8, C. P. 255. Infants and aliens, being men subject to a legal incapacity, cannot be struck off unless objected to ; but women, not being men at all, are in a different position : *Per* Blackburn, J., in *Oldham*, 1 O'M. & H. 159. I do not follow the distinction made by Mr. Justice Blackburn between infants and

"(2.) Is a British subject by birth or naturalization ; (r) ^{Allegiance.} and

" (3.) Is the owner of real property (s) within any city ^{Ownership.} or part of a city [in the electoral district,] of the actual ^{Cities, $300.} value of at least three hundred dollars, or within any town or part of a town [in the electoral district] of the ^{Towns, $200.} actual value of at least two hundred dollars, or in any place in the electoral district, other than a city or town, ^{Other places} of the actual value of at least one hundred and fifty ^{$150.} dollars ; (t) or

" (4.) Is the tenant of any real property within the ^{Tenancy.} electoral district, under a lease, at a monthly rental of at least two dollars, or at a quarterly rental of at least six dollars, or at a half-yearly rental of at least twelve dollars, ^{Rental.} or at an annual rental of at least twenty dollars, (u) and has been in possession thereof as such tenant for at least one year before [his being placed upon the list of voters, or the date of the application for the placing of his name on the list of voters,] (v) and has really and *bona fide*

---

women :   *Per* Lord Coleridge, C. J., in *Stowe* v. *Jolliffe*, L. R. 9, C. P. 743. See further note (o) p. 45, of the original work.

(r) See notes (e) and (f) pp. 59-64, and note (r) p. 82, of the original work.

(s) This incorporates the provisions of sub-ss. (3) of ss. 3 and 4 of the original Act respecting " owners." See notes (g) to (i) to that Act, pp. 64-67, and (s) p. 82, of the original work.

(t) This amendment retains the graduated scales of values for real property for the qualification of owners and occupants, referred to in note (e) p. 67 of the original work.

(u) See pp. 67-72 and 82-84 of the original work.

(v) There was an ambiguity in the original clause, owing to the " period of possession" which was *the year next before the first of January,* not agreeing with the " period of payment," which was for *the year next before the date of*

Payment of rent. paid one year's rent for such real property, at not less than the rate aforesaid ; (w) except when the rental is an annual one and for a larger sum than twenty dollars, in which case it shall be sufficient that at least twenty dollars of the last year's rent which accrued next before the [time aforesaid, (x)] shall have been paid : Provided **As to changes of tenancy.** always, that a change [or changes] of tenancy during the year shall not deprive such tenant of the right to be registered on a list of voters if such change [or changes have been] without any intermission of time [between the tenancies,] and [if] the several tenancies are such as would entitle the tenant to be registered on a list of voters had such tenant been in possession under [any one] of them, as such tenant, for the year next before the

---

the certificate of the final revision of the list. This ambiguity led to some confusion in the terms prescribing the conditions under which a change of tenancies " was not to disqualify a voter." This amendment now makes the two periods either "the year before his being placed upon the list of voters, or the date of the application for the placing of his name on the list of voters," *i. e.*, the year next before (1) *the date of his being placed upon the list* of voters ; or (2) *the date of the application* for the placing of the name on the list of voters ; and adopts these two dates from which the computation of the qualifying year prescribed by this amending Act is to be reckoned. Both dates are variable ; and the terms used are capable of variable constructions, which will be found more fully discussed in note (g) to s. 5 of this amending Act p. 24, *post.*

(w) The following words have been struck out here in the original clause : " Provided that the year's rent, so required to be paid to entitle such tenant to vote shall be the year's rent up to the last yearly, half yearly, quarterly or monthly, day of payment, as the case may be, which shall have occurred next before the date of the certificate of the final revision of the list of voters made by the Revising Officer, as hereinafter mentioned."

(x) "Time aforesaid." The words in the original clause for which these are substituted, were : " date of the said certificate."

[time aforesaid] : (*y*) [Provided also, that in any place except a city, town or incorporated village, the rental hereinbefore mentioned may be payable in money, in kind, or in money's worth of like value ; (*z*)] and provided further, that if on any revised or final assessment roll the amount of the tenant's rent is not stated, the fact that the real property in respect of which his name is entered on such roll as the tenant thereof, is assessed on such roll in cities at three hundred dollars or more, or in towns at two hundred dollars or more, or in any place other than a city or town at one hundred and fifty dollars or more, shall be *prima facie* evidence of his right to be registered on the list of voters, so far as such right depends on the amount of rental (*a*) ; or— As to valuation on assessment roll

" (5.) Is the *bona fide* occupant of real property (*b*) Occupancy. within any city or part of a city in the electoral district, of the actual value of at least three hundred dollars, or within any town or part of a town in the electoral district, of the actual value of at least two hundred dollars, or in any place in the electoral district, other than a city or town, of the actual value of at least one hundred and fifty dollars : (*c*) Provided in every such case, that such As to length of possession.

(*y*) The qualification in respect of the occupation of a house for twelve months is a distinct qualification from the occupation of two houses in succession for twelve months : *Foskett* v. *Kaufman*, 16 Q. B. D. 279. See further note (*g*) p. 71 of the original work.

(*z*) This proviso is taken from sub-s. 4 of s. 4 of the original Act : See note (*v*) p. 84 of the original work.

(*a*) See note (*n*) p. 8, *ante.*

(*b*) See pp. 73-76 and 85-86 of the original work.

(*c*) The amendment here made strikes out the following words : " whether such occupation be under a license of occupation, or agreement to purchase:

person has been in possession of such real property as such occupant for one year next before [his being placed upon the list of voters, or the date of the application for the placing of his name on the list of voters (d)] and is, and has been for such time, in the enjoyment of the revenues and profits thereof; (e) or—

Income and Residence.

"(6.) Is a resident within the electoral district, and derives an income of at least three hundred dollars annually (f) from his earnings [in money or money's worth, or partly in money, and partly in money's **(6).** worth (g)] or from some profession, calling, office or trade, or from some investment in Canada, and has so derived such income and has been a resident [of Canada] for one year next before [his being placed upon the list of voters,

---

from the Crown, or from any other person or corporation, or exists in any other manner except as owner or tenant."

(d) See note (r) *ante* p. 11, and note (g) p. 24 *post.*

(e) The following words have been struck out of the original clause : " for the use of such occupant, or in the case of a married man for his own use or for the use of his wife." The words of limitation in this proviso relating to "possession," and "enjoyment of the revenues and profits " of the qualifying property, in some measure conflict with the definition of "occupant" given in s. 2 of this Act, where the occupant is the wife, and as such entitled to hold her real property as " separate estate " under a marriage settlement, or recent Provincial statutes. The provision in the defining clause as to "occupation" reads : "in his own right, or, in the case of a married man in his own right, or in the right of his wife, or *whose wife is in such actual occupation,* and who or whose wife receives to his or *her own use the revenues and profits thereof.* Similar words of limitation are not attached to the clause giving the property qualification of an owner (p. 6 *ante*). See further notes (a) p. 40, and (x) p. 75 of the original work.

(f) See pp. 76-78 and 79 of the original work.

(g) These words are similar to the words used in the second proviso of subs. (4). See note (r) p. 84 of the original work.

or the date of the application for the placing of his name
on the list of voters (*h*) ;] or—

" (7.) Is a farmer's son not otherwise qualified to vote As a farm-
in the electoral district in which his father's farm is ^{er's son}
situated ; and—

" (*a*) If his father is living, is and has been resident If father is
[within the electoral district] continuously, (*i*) [except ^{living.}

(*h*) The period of residence required of this class of voters is now one year
in " Canada, "—not one year in the Electoral District as required by the
original Act.   Under this clause any person becoming a resident of an
Electoral District immediately before the final revision of the voters' lists
may apply to have his name entered on such lists, if otherwise qualified as
above.   See also note (*v*) p. 11, *ante,* and note (*g*) p. 24, *post.*

(*i*) The former words were " resident continuously on the farm of his father
in such electoral district for one year."   This may be found to be the only
clause which applies to the sons of owners of farms, and to the sons of tenants
of farms under a five years' lease.   The condition as to a year's residence with his
father in the Electoral District may sometimes prevent farmers' and owners' sons
from being registered as voters, as in cases where the father has moved from
one Electoral District to another within the year specified.   The father's title,
if that of owner, may be acquired immediately before the date of the
final revision of the voters' list, and as no period of ownership or residence
is prescribed as a condition of registration in the case of an owner, his name
may be placed on the voter's list at the final revision, provided a proper application for that purpose has been made to the Revising Officer.   But the sons
of such farmer or owner, not having been resident within the Electoral District for the statutory year as above required, cannot be entered on such
voters' list as farmers' sons or owners' sons.   Neither can the tenant of a farm
under a five years' lease, be registered until he has been in possession of the
qualifying farm "as such tenant for at least one year, etc.," (subs. 4), nor
can his sons be registered as farmers' sons until they have been resident
within the Electoral District continuously with their father for one year, etc.
The omission of the words in the original Act : " resident continuously *on*
the farm of his father," from this amendment, leaves untouched the condition
of "actual occupation" contained in the definition of " farm " in the origi-

as hereinafter provided, with] his father for one year next before [his being placed upon the list of voters, or the date of the application for the placing of his name on the list of voters, (j)] if the value of such farm is sufficient, if equally divided among [the father or one or more sons (k)] as co-owners, to qualify them to be registered as voters, in which case the father and such one or more sons as so desire may be so registered as voters ; and if there are more such sons than one resident as aforesaid, and claiming to be registered as voters in respect thereof, and if the value of the farm of the father is not sufficient to give the father and each of such sons the right to vote in respect of such value, if equally divided among them, then the right to be registered as a voter and to vote in respect of such farm, shall belong only to the father and the eldest or so many of the elder of such sons, being so resident as aforesaid, as the value of such farm, if equally divided, will qualify ; or

Value to be apportioned in case of more than one son.

---

nal Act. The above clause is not free from doubt as to its applicability to the sons of tenant-farmers, owing to the definition of the term "farm" being still retained, and also owing to certain other phraseology retained in the clause. See note (g) p. 44, and the notes on "actual occupation" pp. 33, 72-74, of the original work.

(j) See note (v) p. 11, *ante* and note (g) p. 24, *post.*

(k) "The value of such farm." Although it is not stated whether the "value" in the case of the sons of tenant-farmers is to be according to the rental value or the real value, it must be presumed that the qualifying value applicable to the father's property is to govern in determining the right of the sons to vote,—i.e., the rental value as prescribed by sub-s. 4 pp. 11-13 *ante.* The amendment by which the words within brackets are substituted for the word "them" makes it clear that the father's name must be entered on the voters' list, as stated in note (h) p. 80 of the original work.

" (*b*) If his father is dead, is and has been resident *If father is dead.* [within the electoral district] continuously, (*l*) [except as hereinafter provided, with] his father or [with] his mother (after the death of his father) being the owner [of the farm, in respect of which the right of voting is claimed *Mother being the owner of farm.* by or for him (*m*)] for one year next before [his being placed upon the list of voters, or the date of the applica-

---

(*l*) See notes pp. 80 and 89 of the original work and note (*i*) p. 15 *ante.*

(*m*) "Mother being the *owner* of the farm in respect of which the right of voting is claimed by or for him." The difficulty of applying the above sub-section to the case of tenant-farmers' sons, where the mother is *tenant* of the farm under a five years' lease, has been referred to in note (*k*) p. 8 *ante.* The title of the class whose sons may be registered under this sub-s. is plainly designated to be that of *owner* ; and is the same term as is used in sub-s. 8 (*b*) p. 20 *post*, defining the right of "owners' sons," where the mother is the "owner" after the death of the father. The qualifying property is termed a "farm," which is defined to be "land actually *occupied by the owner thereof*, and not less in quantity than twenty acres ; and ' farmer ' means such *owner* thereof." And if the sons of tenants are to be registered under this clause, it is clear that the words "*or tenant*," should be imported or inserted after the word "owner,"—so that the clause may read : " being the owner *or tenant* of the farm in respect of which the right of voting is claimed." Whether such a construction would come within the prohibition of "judge-made law," must be determined after a consideration of the whole Act and the rules as to the construction and interpretation of statutes, referred to in notes (*v*) p. 84, (*u*) p. 165 of the original work. Where the intention of the Legislature can be collected from the statute itself, words may be modified, altered or supplied in the statute so as obviate any repugnancy to, or inconsistency with, such intention : *Quin* v. *O'Keefe*, 10 Ir. C. L. R. 393. "If upon the face of the Act of Parliament you find that giving the ordinary sense and meaning to the words, you are involved in some inconsistency in any of the other clauses, it may then be necessary to search about and see whether the palpable and obvious construction which the words point at may not be varied in order that the inconsistency may be avoided : " *Per* Lord Hatherley in *Green* v. *Rey.*, 1 Ap. Cas. 552. " A judge may take the view that a section in an Act as it stands

3

tion for the placing of his name on the list of voters (*n*)]
if the value of the farm, [in respect of which it is claimed
that he should be registered as a voter] is sufficient, if
equally divided among all the sons of such father as co-
owners (*o*) to qualify them as voters under this Act, in
which case such one or more sons as so desire may be so
Case of more registered as voters ; and if there are more such sons than
than one son. one resident as aforesaid, and claiming to be registered as

---

is so absurd that a certain word in it cannot stand there ; but that does not
quite conclude that you can insert another word. A Judge may take the
view that there is sufficient in the section and some of the following sections
to enable him to insert another word." *Per* Sir G. Jessel, M.R., in *Laird* v.
Briggs, 19 Ch. D. 33. "The term 'judge-made law' would seem to denote law
made by subject judges, as opposed to law made by the sovereign legislature.
At least it would seem to denote law made by subject-judges as ex-
pressing their judicial functions.   Provided it be made in the direct or legislative manner, law, established immediately by subject judges, is
just as good as law emanating immediately from the Sovereign :"
Austin's Jurisprudence, 549. "Notwithstanding the clearness and the pre-
cision with which the law-giver conceives and expresses his actual intention
or purpose, the statute may be fitted imperfectly to accomplish the end or
purpose by which ho is determined to make it. And hence the spurious
interpretation *ex ratione legis*, through which a statute unequivocally worded
by the law-giver, is extended or restricted by the Judge. By such extensive
or restricted interpretation the Judge may depart from the manifest sense of
a statute, in order that he may carry into effect its *ratio* or scope. But in
these cases, he is not a *Judge* properly interpreting the law, but a *legislator*
correcting its errors or defects. He supposes the expressions which the law-
giver would have used. And these supposed expressions he substitutes for
the clear expressions which the law-giver has actually used. This, however,
is not *interpretation*, but a process of legislative amendment, or a process of
legislative correction, which lays all statute law at the arbitrary disposition
of the tribunals :" *Ibid* 650. See also the amended s. 8, p. 23 *post.*

(*n*) See notes (*v*) p. 11 *ante*, and (*y*) p. 24 *post.*

(*o*) "Sons of such father as co-owners." This clause is intended to give
the right of voting to the farmers' sons who have been resident with

voters in respect therof, (*p*) and if the value of such farm
is not sufficient to give each of such sons the right to vote
in respect of such value, if equally divided among them, Value to be
apportioned.
then the right to be registered as a voter and to vote in
respect of such farm shall belong only to the eldest or so
many of the elder of such sons, being so resident as aforesaid, as the value of such farm, if equally divided, will
qualify ; or—

" (8.) Is the son of an owner of real property (*q*) in As son of
owner not a
such electoral district, or portion of an electoral district, farmer.
other than a farm, and is otherwise qualified to vote
(*r*) in the electoral district in which such property is
situated ; and—

" (*a*) If his father is living, is and has been resident If father is
living.
[within the electoral district (*s*)] continuously, [except as
hereinafter provided] with his father for one year next
before [his being placed upon the list of voters, or the

---

their father on the farm, during his lifetime, and subsequently with their
mother on such farm, after the death of the father. After the death of the
father, their right depends upon the mother having the title in herself, and
upon the sons being "not otherwise qualified to vote in the Electoral
District." The phrase : " if equally divided among all the sons of such
father as co-owners," does not aid in construing this clause as applicable to
the case of the sons of tenant-farmers referred to in note (*m*) p. 17 *ante*. See
further notes (*e*) p. 78, (*l*) p. 80, and (*g*) p. 88, of the original work.

(*p*) The amendment makes a slight change in the wording of the
original clause, but does not vary the sense of it.

(*q*) The statutory qualifications of farmers' sons and owners' sons are the
same; and the distinction between the two classes of voters is in name only,
except that, under this Act, the sons of tenant-farmers have been added to
the franchise. See notes (*k*) p. 16 and (*m*) p 17 *ante*.

(*r*) See notes (*f*) p. 79 of the original work.

(*s*) See notes (*i*) p. 15 *ante*.

date of the application for the placing of his name on the list of voters, (*t*)] if the value of the real property on which his father resides (*u*) and in respect of which his father is qualified to be registered as a voter as owner, is sufficient, if equally divided among the father and one or more sons as co-owners, to qualify them to be registered as voters under this Act, in which case the father and such one or more sons as so desire, may be so registered as voters; [and if there are more such sons than one resident as aforesaid, and claiming to be registered as voters in respect of such property,] and if the value thereof is not sufficient to give the father and each of the sons the right to vote in respect of such value, if equally divided, (*v*) then the right to be registered as a voter and to vote in respect of such real property, shall belong only to the father and the eldest or so many of the elder of such sons, being so resident as aforesaid, as the value of such real property, if equally divided, will qualify; or—

Value to be apportioned in the case of more than one son.

If father is dead.   "(*b*) If his father is dead, is and has been resident [within the electoral district] continuously, [except as hereinafter provided] with his father, or with his mother (after the death of his father) being such owner, for one year next before [his being placed upon the list of voters,

***

(*t*) See note (*v*) p. 11 *ante*, and note (*g*) to s. 5, p. 24 *post*.

(*u*) The omission from this, and the subs. defining the qualifications of farmers' sons, of the words "resident upon the property," and "resident on the farm," makes no substantial variation in the condition of actual residence on the qualifying property. See the latter part of note (*i*) p. 15, *ante*.

(*v*) These words make the intention of the provision in the original Act more clear.

or the date of the application for the placing of his name on the list of voters,] if the value of the real property on which his father, or his mother (after the death of his father) resided or resides, and in respect of which such father would, if living, be qualified to be registered as a voter as owner, is sufficient, if equally divided among all his sons as co-owners, to qualify them to be registered as voters under this Act, in which such case such one or more sons as so desire may be so registered as voters ; [and if there are more such sons than one resident as aforesaid, and claiming to be registered as voters in respect of such property,] and if the value thereof is not sufficient to give each of such sons the right to vote in respect of such value, if equally divided, then the right to be registered as a voter and to vote in respect of such real property, shall belong only to the eldest or so many of the elder of such sons, being so resident as aforesaid, as the value of such real property, if equally divided, will qualify ; (*w*) or—

Case of more than one son.

Value to be apportioned.

"(9.) Is a fisherman, resident in the electoral district, (*x*) and is the owner of real property and boats, nets, fishing gear, and tackle, within any such electoral district, [or portion of an electoral district, or of a share or shares

As a fisherman.

(*w*) See the notes to the clauses defining the qualifications of farmers' sons, pp. 15-19 *ante.*

(*x*) As intimated in note (*o*) to the original clause (subs. 9, s. 4) p. 90, "the fisherman franchise" was not extended to cities and towns. The effect of this amendment is to make the above franchise of general application to all Electoral Districts. No period of residence prior to the revision of the voters' lists is required for this franchise. Fishermen who are "tenants" or "occupants" are not entitled to be registered as voters under this clause.

in a registered ship (y)] which together are of the actual value of at least one hundred and fifty dollars; or—

As annuitant and resident.

" [(10.) Is and has been, for one year next before his being placed upon the list of voters, or the date of the application for the placing of his name on the list of voters, a resident within the electoral district, and in receipt of a life annuity secured on real estate in Canada, by virtue of a deed of donation or any other title equivalent thereto, of at least one hundred dollars in money or money's worth, or partly in money and partly in money's worth."(z)]

S. 5 repealed; new provision.

3. Section five of the said Act is hereby repealed and the following substituted therefor :—

Qualifications of voters in a city or town, and in a county or riding.

" 5. The qualifications required of voters [in respect of a city or town, or portion of a city or town] shall apply to voters in respect of a city or town, or a portion of a city or town attached for electoral purposes to a county

---

(y) This extends the franchise to "fishermen" who are owners of shares in a registered ship; *i.e.*, a ship registered under the Merchant Shipping Acts, and who are also owners of real property.

(z) This clause adds a new class of votes not hitherto included in any Provincial franchise. The qualifications for this class are :

(1) Being a resident of the Electoral District for one year ; and

(2) Being in receipt of an annuity of at least $100 in money or money's worth, or partly in both, —

(a) Secured on real estate,

(b) By a deed of donation, or other title equivalent thereto.

Under a will creating a charge on lands for support and maintenance during life, the chargee takes no legal estate in such lands : *Gilchrist* v. *Ramsay*, 27 U. C. Q. B. 500. See further *Fisken* v. *Brooke*, 4 App. R. 8. See as to the period of residence required prior to the revision of the voters' list, note (g) p. 24 *post*.

or riding of a county in any electoral district; and the qualifications required of voters [in respect of any place other than a city or town] shall apply to voters in respect of any municipality or place, not being a city or town or a portion of a city or town, which is attached to or included for electoral purposes in a city or town or portion of a city or town." (a)

4. Sections one, two, three and twelve of this Act shall not come into force until the first day of January, in the year one thousand eight hundred and eighty-seven. *When certain sections shall come into force.*

5. Section eight of the said Act is hereby repealed and the following substituted therefor:— *S. 8 repealed; new provision.*

"**8.** In the case of a farmer's son or of the son of an owner of real property other than a farmer, each such son, to entitle him to vote as such, under the foregoing provisions of this Act (b) [must have been, from the time of his name having been placed on the list of voters to the time of the election for the electoral district in which he tenders his vote, (c)] and must then be, a resident in such electo- *As to residence of persons qualified as sons.*

(a) The only amendment made to the original section is to strike out the references to ss. 3 and 4, and to adapt it to the consolidation of these sections in s. 2 of this Act.

(b) This new section is a consolidation and amendment of the provisoes to subs. 3 of s. 3 ; subss. 7 and 8 of s. 4, and of s. 8 of the original Act.

(c) The amendments provide : (1) That the voter must be a resident in the Electoral District with his father (or mother) "from the time of his name been placed on the list of voters to the time of the election ;" and (2) at the time of the election. They also provide that "occasional absence" (1) for six months in the year before his being placed on the list of voters ; and (2) for six months subsequent to the then last revision of such list shall not disqualify. These two periods of six months each may, in some cases, practically annihilate the "year" of residence.

ral district (*d*) as hereinbefore provided with his father, (or with his mother after the death of his father), being such owner (*e*) as aforesaid; but—

Occasional
absence.

"(*a*) Occasional absence or absences (*f*) of any such son from the residence of his father (or of his mother, as the case may be), for any period or periods not exceeding in all six months in the year [next before his being placed on the list of voters, or the date of the application for pla-

Prior to and
subsequent
to revision.

cing his name on the said list, or for any period or periods not exceeding in all six months subsequent to the then last revision of such list (*g*)] shall not disqualify such son from being placed on the list of voters, or from voting :—

(*d*) The cases as to "residence" in the notes on pp. 74, 76 and 97 to the original work, give the legal definitions and meanings of the terms "resident" and "residence;" but whether a particular person is or is not a "resident" is a question of fact to be proved by evidence, and a question of law depending upon that evidence.

(*e*) "Being such owner." See notes (*m*) p. 17, and (*o*) p. 18 *ante*.

· (*f*) The term "occasional absence" must be defined by the Revising Officer as a question of law. "Occasional" is defined to mean : "incidental, casual, occurring at times, but not regular or systematic." It may be said to be the converse of "continuous," or "permanent." See further note (*j*) p. 101 of the original work.

(*g*) The periods here substituted for those in the original Act have been referred to in note (*v*) to this Act, p. 11 *ante*. Each period is capable of being construed so as to fix variable dates for the computation of the qualifying year. The expression, "the year next before his being placed on the list of voters," may be construed to mean either : (1) The date of actual entry by the Revising Officer of such person's name on the preliminary list of voters ; or (2) The first publication of such list with such person's name "placed on the list ;" or (3) The placing of such person's name on the list at the sitting for the preliminary, or for the final, revision ; or (4) The date of the certificate of the final revision with the name of such person finally "placed on the list." A key to the interpretation of the period first mentioned in the Act: "the year next before his being placed on the list of voters," is furnished by the last clause of the oaths (C D E or F) to be taken by farmers' and owners' sons at elections, which provides for and allows occasional absence subsequent to the final revision: "I have not been absent from such residence more than six months *since I was placed on the list of voters* ;" and also by the words interpreting this clause of the oath and authorizing such absence, which read in subsection (a) of this clause : "six months *subsequent to the then last revision of such list.*" This expression "placed on the list of voters," being the same as that used in other sections of this Act, may therefore receive the same construction ; and if so then the date of "being placed on the list of voters," would be the same as the date of the "then last revision of such list," from which the qualifying year of residence should be computed. In a Dominion Election case it was held by the Election Court that the elector's oath could be referred as aiding in the construction of the clause respecting the qualification of voters : *North Victoria,* H. E. C. 611. The other period named in these amendments is " the date of the application for the placing of his name on the list ;" and may mean either the *date* (1) of the written notice of application (Form E p. 176 of the original work) ; or (2) of the hearing of such application, on (a) the preliminary, or (b) the final, revision of the list of voters. A claimant may apply at both revisions to be placed on the list of voters ; and the Revising Officer may at the preliminary revision either reject the application, or adjourn it to the final revision. A rejection at the preliminary revision is not necessarily a bar to an application at the final revision ; for it would be discretionary with the Revising Officer to allow a second application ; and he would be bound to do so if the claimant became otherwise qualified in the meantime. The form of oath in cases where the application has been refused (form G *post*), and where an appeal is pending,—if there were no other words to guide in reading the clause,—might throw some doubt on the construction above suggested. The latter oath requires the voter to swear to a different period of absence to that allowed by the words, ''six months *since my first application be placed on the list of voters,*"—not since ''*the then last revision of such list*" as allowed in subs. (a) of the above clause of this Act. But the rule for the construction of statutes in such cases is, that if the enacting part of the Act and the forms given in the schedule, cannot be made to correspond, the latter must yield to the former : *Re Barnes* 1 Cr. & Ph. 46 ; *Dean* v. *Green* 8 P. D. 89, and note (a) p. 176 and note (b) p. 127 of the original work. There is, however, no clear authority to guide the Revising

4

Certain time to be deemed as spent at home.

"(b) And the time spent by such son as a mariner or as a fisherman, in the pursuit of either of the said occupations, or as a student at any institution of learning in Canada, shall be considered, for the purposes of this Act, as having been spent at the residence of his father, or of his mother, as the case may be." (h)

Time and place for final revision of voters' list.

6. The time to be fixed for the final revision of lists of voters under the said Act, shall be not less than five weeks after the publication by posting up of the lists, (i) and each sitting for such final revision shall include, when practicable, at least three and (except in cities and towns) not more than five polling districts; the place for the holding of the final revision shall be in one of the polling districts the lists for which are to be so finally revised; and there shall be a sitting for such final revision in each city, town, township, parish, incorporated village, and

---

Officer as to which construction he may adopt in fixing the period first mentioned ; and a ruling by one officer will not be binding upon another. Nor would a Revising Officer be bound in all cases to follow his previous rulings. The Court of Common Pleas, though a court of ultimate appeal in registration cases, will review its previous decisions when clearly erroneous : *Hadfield's Case* L. R. 8 C. P, 306. " I should be sorry to lay it down as rule that the Court cannot depart from a previous decision, especially when it is shewn that there has been an omission to cite an earlier authority, or a clear mistake in its application :" Per Bovill, C. J., *Ibid* 313. " Wherever a new jurisdiction is given to the Courts some time must necessarily elapse before the law can be settled ; and great inconvenience and mischief must result if the Courts were absolutely bound by their decisions, though manifestly erroneous :" *Ibid.*

(h) This clause was section 8 in the original Act.

(i) This provision is the same as that in the first part of s. 26 of the original Act. See note (j) p. 136 of the original work.

other known territorial division, (*j*) and in the province
of Prince Edward Island at least two sittings in each
existing provincial electoral district except Charlottetown
and Royalty, and Georgetown and Royalty.

7. The Revising Officer shall exhibit to any person re- Notices of additions, quiring to examine the same, all notices of additions or &c., to be exhibited on objections or declarations in support thereof, deposited request. with or mailed to him under sections nineteen and twenty-
six of the said Act, and shall permit copies thereof to be
taken. (*k*)

(*j*) This alters the provisions of ss. 26 and 48 of the original Act, and
makes provision as to the places where the Revision Courts are to be held for
the final revision.   But the meaning of the provision is not very clear.
The first part provides that not less than three, and not more than five, polling
districts may be grouped together for the final Revision Court, except in cities
and towns, where the number of grouped polling districts may exceed five.
The latter part of the clause provides that " there shall be *a sitting in each*
city, town, township, parish, incorporated village, and other known territorial
division," which would seem to conflict with the first part of the section in cases
where such municipal or territorial division (except cities and towns) com-
prised more than five polling districts.   Besides, some of the cities comprise
several Electoral Districts , and the revision for each such Electoral District
must take place within its defined limits.   It is obvious that outside his Electoral district the Revising Officer would have no jurisdiction to hold a court
or sitting for the revision of the lists.   So where municipal townships have
been divided for electoral purposes the one sitting in such township would not
comply with the intentions of the original Act.   See note (*m*) on the construction and interpretation of ambiguous clauses in Acts of Parliament, p. 17,
ante.

(*k*) This is supplementary to the directions contained in s. 56 of the original Act, which require the Revising Officer to keep certain documents in his
office "open for inspection by any one desiring to inspect the same."   The
common law rule is that where documents are of a public nature, and are
kept for the use of the public at large, every person affected or interested in
such documents has a right to inspect them at reasonable times.   Statutes

prescribing such right of inspection are supplementary of the common law. Documents which are of a public nature and which are public documents cannot be withheld from inspection: *Rex* v. *Bishop of Ely,* 8 B. & C. 112. The right to inspect may be enforced by *mandamus: Tapping on Mandamus,* 94, 161. And when a new right has been created by Act of Parliament the proper method of enforcing it is by *mandamus* at common law : *Simpson* v. *Scottish Union &c., Co.,* 1 Hem. & Mil. 618, s. c. 9 Jur. N. S. 711. The writ lies to allow a burgess to inspect the voting papers deposited with a town clerk, and to compare them with a list of his own, and to permit him to mark on such list the information he finds in such]papers : *Rex* v. *Arnold,* 4 A. & E. 657. An inhabitant of a parish and interested in the question of a custom as to a church rate may have liberty to inspect the parish books : *Anon.* 2 Chit R., 290. A rated parishioner has an interest in seeing what has been done with the corporate funds, and whether the expenditure of the parish money is proper. And without any statutory provision authorizing inspection, the Court will grant him a *mandamus* to inspect the accounts of such expenditure : *Rex* v. *Great Farrington,* 9 B. & C. 541. But he must show that the purpose for which he desires the inspection is one connected with the general interest of the public and not arising out of his own personal convenience or caprice : *Rex* v. *Clear,* 7 Dow. & L. 393. And it will not be granted to ratepayers merely to gratify a rational curiosity after the accounts have been audited and published : *Rex* v. *Staffordshire,* 6 A. & E. 84. " We are by no means disposed to narrow our own authority to enforce by *mandamus* the production of every document of a public nature in which any one of the King's subjects can prove himself to be interested. For such persons, every officer appointed by law to keep records ought to deem himself a trustee :" *Per* Lord Denman, C.J., *Ibid* 99. " I do not see upon what principle of justice he who is a trustee and guardian of the evidence of other's rights can lock it up from them :" *Per* Lord Ellenborough, C.J., in *Rex* v. *Tower,* 4 Mau. & Sel. 162. A resident inhabitant of a corporate town, though not a corporator, but who is living in a place in which he is under the rule and government of the corporation, may have an inspection of their by-laws : *Harrison* v. *Williams,* 4 Dow. & Ry. 820. The writ will be granted in the case of a private corporation to inspect a book of accounts between the company and its shareholders, and which is regarded as confidential : *People* v. *Pacific Mail Steamship Co.,* 50 Barb. 280. And to aid a judgment creditor of a company in ascertaining who are its shareholders and the amounts unpaid by them : *Reg.* v. *Derbyshire,* 3 E. & B. 784. Everybody has a right to inspect the books of the sessions of a 'corporation :

8. If at the time of the final revision the person by whom any application to add to, amend or correct the list was made, or notice of any objection or complaint was given, does not appear in support of the application, objection or complaint, or is desirous of withdrawing the same, (*l*) the Revising Officer shall allow any other elector, who is so desirous of so doing, to appear in support of such application, objection or complaint, or he may, without such substitution, hear any evidence that is available in support thereof and dispose of the matter accordingly. (*m*)

Provision in case of withdrawal of objection.

Substitute.

9. The Revising Officer shall not remove the name of any person entered on the list of voters from such list on

Person objected to not

Herbert v. *Ashburner*, 1 Wils. 297. In determining the right of persons to inspect all papers relating to the voters' list, it must be remembered that the right of voting at Parliamentary Elections exists for the benefit of the whole people and not for the benefit of the individual voter. See notes (*a*) p. 13, and (*b*) p. 157, of the original work. Our laws treat the elective franchise as a sacred trust, committed only to that portion of the citizens who come up to the prescribed standards of qualification : *Brightly on Elections*, 230. When a person gives a notice of objections to a voters' list he places himself in the position of a public officer : *Proudfoot* v. *Barnes*, L. R. 2 C. P. 88. Proceedings affecting voters' lists are not a mere private privilege, but a matter of public concern : *Re Simpson and the Judge of Lanark*, 9 Pr. R. 358.

(*l*) This is similiar to section 19 of the Ontario Voters' List Act, R. S. O. ch. 9 ; except that the latter Act provides that in case the appellant or complainant dies pending the hearing of his complaint, the County Judge may allow any other person qualified to be appellant or complainant to intervene and prosecute the appeal or complaint. See notes (*h*) p. 125 and (*l*) p. 136, of the original work.

(*m*) Under this power it will be competent for any counsel or agent of a political organization to conduct the proceedings instituted by an absent appellant or complainant. The representative however should appear " in support of " the pending application. See note (*x*) p. 166 of the original work.

to be remov-
ed if other-
◆ se qualified

the ground that the qualification of such person is incorrectly entered thereon, if it appears that such person is entitled to be registered on the list of voters as possessed of any of the qualifications set forth in the said Act, but the Revising Officer shall retain the name of such person on the list and correct the same accordingly. (*n*)

s. 33 repeal-
ed ; new pro-
vision.

10. Section thirty-three of the said Act is hereby repealed, and the following substituted therefor : (*o*)

(*n*) This power may be exercised on an application to strike out the name of the voter on the ground of his not having the qualification entered on the voters' list. Whether the amendment can be made on an *ex parte* application at any sitting of the Revision Court, is questionable. The words used in this section infer an application to the Revising Officer to strike off the name from the list of voters, viz. : "shall not remove the name of any person" *on the ground* that the qualification of such person is incorrectly entered on the list if it appears that such person is otherwise qualified. Where a qualification of a voter appears to be good according to the entries on the voters' list, and though in fact the voter is not possessed of such qualification, the Revising Barrister cannot take notice of that fact unless the vote has been duly objected to by a properly qualified person : *Smith* v. *James*, L. R. 1 C. P. 138. The following observations apply to the Act 6 Vic. ch. 18 (Imp.) "The power of altering the qualification was taken away from the Revising Barrister in order to hold the scale fairly and evenly, so far as possible, between the objector and the voter : Because, otherwise if a person should come and claim at the Revising Court in respect of a qualification which was a wholly different one from that described in the list, the objector would be taken by surprise and would have no fair opportunity of supporting his objection or, of previously inquiring as to whether his objection was valid or not :" *Per* Lord Esher, M.R., in *Foskett* v. *Kaufman*, 16 Q. B. D. 288. The case of a misnomer on the voters' list is not provided for in this section ; but the form of the oath at the polls will protect a voter improperly named on such voters' list. See further pp. 116, 118, 120, of the original work, and *Foskett* v. *Kaufman*, 16 Q. B. D. 279, and *Dashwood* v. *Ayles, Ibid.* 295.

(*o*) The amendments made to this section are : (1) altering the date of the commencement of the proceedings for the revision of the voters' lists from

" **33.** On or as soon as possible after the first day of June (*p*) in each year after the year of Our Lord one thousand eight hundred and eighty-six, the Revising Officer, being duly sworn as hereinbeforo provided, shall cause the list of voters of the preceding year to be compared with the last assessment rolls, (*q*) and shall, with all the information that he can obtain from that or any other source, proceed to revise the lists of voters then in force under this Act for the electoral district or portion of an electoral district for which he is appointed, entering thereupon the names of all persons not already on

Proceedings to review future lists.

---

the 1st January to the 1st June in each year ; and (2) striking out the words which required the Revising Officer to be guided by "the last revised or final" assessment roll.

(*p*) Under the original Act the Revising Officers were required to commence their annual proceedings for the revision of the voters' lists after the 1st January ; to publish such lists on or before the 1st March ; to certify the preliminary revision of such lists on or before the 1st May ; to publish such lists on or before the 1st June ; and to forward the finally revised lists to the Clerk of the Crown in Chancery on or before the 1st August.   This Act requires the Revising Officers to commence their annual work of revision after the 1st June ; to certify and publish the lists on or before the 1st September ; and to forward the finally revised lists to the Clerk of the Crown in Chancery on or before the 1st November.   The effect of the amendment is to make the voters' lists prepared in 1886 valid until "on or before the 1st November, 1887."   See further the notes to the original work, pp. 113, 120 and 147.

(*q*) The changes here made direct the Revising Officer to cause the lists of the preceding year to be compared with the assessment roll, instead of directing him to procure copies of "the *last revised or final* assessment roll," or voters' lists ; "and with such copies and such other information as can be obtained " to proceed to revise the list for the year.   This amendment makes the assessment roll, after it has been completed and returned by the Assessors, and before it has been revised by the Municipal Court of Revision, the foundation of the Revising Officer's proceedings.

What the lists shall show.

such lists, and who, according to the provisions of this Act, are entitled to have their names so entered, indicating in the proper column thereof whether they are qualified in respect of real property, as owners, tenants, occupants, (r) or otherwise, and stating the numbers of the lots, portions of lots and concessions, streets, or other available description of real property in respect of which they are qualified, and their post office addresses as nearly as can be ascertained by the said officer, or whether they are qualified in respect of income; and as to the sons of farmers, or other owners' sons as afore-

Residence Post Office.

said, and voters on income, stating also in such lists in the proper column thereof the residence and post office addresses of such persons as nearly as can be ascertained by him, and noting on the said lists the names of any persons who are dead or who are not, according to the provisions of this Act, entitled to be registered as voters, stating the reason of such note, and making any other

Attestation of changes.

verbal or clerical corrections which seem necessary; and he shall attest all such additions, erasures or corrections, with his initials, and sign such lists as such Revising

Assessment Rolls to be evidence of value.

Officer; and such assessment rolls as aforesaid shall be *prima facie* evidence of value."

S. 42 amended.

11. Section forty-one of the said Act is hereby amended by striking out the words "two hundred" in the third line thereof and inserting the words "three hundred" in lieu thereof. (s)

(r) The following words have been struck out of this part of the original section : "purchasers in occupation under the Crown."

(s) The section amended as above provides for the alteration of polling districts on an increase of voters ; but the difficulty of observing the directions

12. The following are hereby added to section forty-two of the said Act, as sub-sections two and three thereof:

S. 42 amended.

"2. Every person (*t*) in respect of the placing of whose name on the list of voters an application has been made, or notice of an objection or complaint has been given, and every person who gives notice of any such objection or complaint, (*u*) shall, if he is resident within the polling district, the list for which is sought to be amended, or within ten miles thereof, and is not absent from such limits upon being served with a summons (*v*) in the said

Parties if summoned to obey the summons.

When no fees payable.

---

given in the section, and referred to in note (*t*) p. 154 of the original work, has not been remedied by any of the amendments to this Act.

(*t*) In the Ontario Voter's List Act, R. S. O c. 9 s. 10, there is a similar provision for the attendance of persons whose right to vote is questioned before a county judge. Under that Act, the persons must be "resident within the municipality;" but under this Act the person must be a resident of the polling district, or within ten miles of such polling district. The affidavit of service should show where the service was effected; and if the service was made within the ten-mile limit, it should also state the distance of the place of service from the limits of the polling district as affecting, the question of w   ess fees.

(*u*) The notice of objection or complaint which the original Act authorizes may be a written, or a printed, notice. By the *Interpretation Act*, (31 Vic. c. 1 s. 7 subs. 12) it is provided that, "in every Act of the Parliament of Canada the words 'writing' or 'written,' or any term of like import, shall include words printed, painted, engraved, lithographed, or otherwise traced or copied." See further the suggestion of Lord Coleridge, C. J., in *Re Stephens* L. R. 9 C. P. 188 that "photographic copies" of documents might be used in some cases in place of the originals.

(*v*) "Is not absent from such limits." It is not clear whether these words refer to an "absence from such limits" at the time of the service of the summons, or at the time of the holding of the court to which the party affected has been summoned. As non-obedience to the summons subjects

5

form J, (*w*) obey the same without being tendered or paid any allowance for his expenses :

" 3. If any person summoned as in the next preceding sub-section provided, does not so attend in obedience to such summons, (*x*) the Revising Officer may, in the absence of satisfactory evidence as to the reason of such non-attendance, (*y*) or, * (*z*) if such person is an applicant to be

Sic.

---

the party to a penalty, an interpretation which is most favourable to the liberty of the subject should be adopted : *Dean* v. *Green*, 8 P. D. 89.

(*w*) The service must be personal ; service by post, or upon a grown up person at the residence of the party summoned, is not sufficient. The original writ of subpœna, under the seal of the Court, or the original order with the signature of the judge, must be shown to the witness at the time of the service and delivery to him of the copy of the subpœna or order : *Smith* v. *Truscott*, 6 M. & Gr. 267. See further note (*w*) p. 155 of the original work.

(*x*) In the case of the non-attendance of the party summoned the Revising Officer must be satisfied (1) that the service of the summons has been personal ; (2) that the original was exhibited to the party served at the time of such service ; (3) if the witness fees have not been paid, that such service was made within the polling district or within ten miles of the limits of such polling district ; (4) that the person served " is not absent from such limits " (see note (*v*) p. 33 *ante*) ; or (5) if the fees have been paid or tendered, that a sufficient amount, as required by the original Act, has been so paid or tendered, (see note (*y*) p. 156 of the original work) ; (6) that the party so served has not attended pursuant to such summons. See as to the right to cross-examine claimants or objectors, note (*s*) p. 14, of the original work.

(*y*) Evidence as to the reason of such non-attendance. See notes (*v*) p. 50, and (*o*) and (*p*) p. 130 of the original work.

(*z*) " Or " seems to be superfluous, unless it can be read " and ; " see the latter part of note (*p*) on p. 29 of the original work. For all purposes of the construction of the section it might be struck out. " It is a canon of construction that, if it be possible, effect must be given to every word of an Act

placed on the list of voters, as to his right to be placed on such list, dismiss the objection or complaint, or strike the name of such person off the list of voters, or refuse to place his name thereon, (*a*) as the case requires ; or the Revising Officer may impose a fine not exceeding five dollars on such *Fine $5.* person, or he may do both." (*b*)

---

of Parliament or other document ; but that if there be a word or a phrase therein to which no sensible meaning can be given, it must be eliminated :" *Per* Brett, J., in *Stone* v. *Yeovil*, 1 C. P. D. 701 ; S. C., 2 C. P. D. 99.

(*a*) But for this provision the Revising Officer would have no jurisdiction in case of the non-attendance of the party as above mentioned, to try the claims or objections made. Where a County Court cause was adjourned for the attendance of a witness, and on the day of the adjournment the plaintiff did not appear, but the Judge at the instance of the defendant tried the cause, and entered a verdict for the defendant : *Held*, that he had no jurisdiction to do so, and that he should have ordered the cause to be struck out : *Jordon* v. *Jones*, 44 J. P. 800 ; 2 Fisher's (Mews) Dig. 1464. When the non-attendance of the person summoned is the result of mere neglect, *i.e.*, "absence of satisfactory evidence as to the reason of such non-attendance," then, if he claims a right to vote, a reasonable punishment would be his temporary loss of the franchise, by the omission of his name from the voters' list for the year ; or if he objects to names on the list, a dismissal of his complaint. But when his non-attendance is wilful, a fact which can only be determined after he has had notice of the charge and an opportunity of answering it, the punishment may also extend to the imposition of a fine. See pp. 128, 140, 143, 155, and 158 of the original work.

(*b*) This is in addition to the power given by section 42 of the original Act : "in the event of such person not attending after being served with such summons the Revising Officer may punish such person as for a contempt of a Court of Record." In addition to the powers conferred by these two sections the Revising Officer has by section 28 of the original Act all the powers of a Court of Record. All Courts of Record have power to fine and imprison for any contempt committed in the face of the Court. But an inferior Court of Record has no power to fine or imprison for a contempt committed out of Court, as the writing and publication of articles in a newspaper reflecting

S. 48 repeal-
ed.   **13.** Section forty-eight of the said Act is hereby
repealed. (c)

Form B
substituted
for form A in
former Act.   **14.** The form B in the schedule to the said Act is
hereby repealed and the form A in the schedule hereto
substituted in lieu thereof. (d)

Time for
future revi-
sions and re-
turns.   **15.** As respects lists of voters revised after the year
one thousand eight hundred and eighty-six, the same shall
be certified and published, in the manner required by
the said Act as hereby amended, on or before the first
day of September in each year, and shall be finally
revised and certified and duplicates thereof forwarded to
the Clerk of the Crown in Chancery on or before the first
day of November in each year. (e)

Revising
Officer un-
able to at-
tend clerk
may adjourn.   **16.** Whenever from illness or from other casualty a
Revising Officer is unable to hold any sitting at the time
appointed therefor, the clerk may adjourn the sitting to
any hour on the day following to be named by him, and
so from day to day until the Revising Officer is able to

---

upon the conduct of the Judge; such contempt may be punished by indict-
ment or otherwise : *Reg.* v. *Lefroy*, L. R. 8 Q. B. 134. See notes on pp.
143 and 155 of the original work.

(c) The section repealed provided for the holding of the Revision Courts
in a central place in each town or village instead of each polling division.
See pp. 162. 163 of the original work. Section 6 of this Act is intended to
make other provisions : see note (j) p. 27 *ante.*

(d) The substituted form is partly taken from that provided by the
Ontario Voters' List Act, R. S. O. ch. 9, as amended by 42 Vic. 3, and 48
Vic. c. 3, s. 3.

(e) See note (p) p. 31 *ante.*

attend, or until other provision is made for the holding
of such sitting. (*f*)

17. Any Revising Officer appointed under the Act hereby amended may, in case of illness or necessary absence, after leave granted therefor by the Governor in Council, appoint a Deputy Revising Officer to act for him during such illness or absence; (*g*) such appointment shall be subject to the approval of the Governor in Council : (*h*)

Deputy may be appointed in certain cases.

2. The Deputy Revising Officer shall be possessed of all the qualifications, (*i*) and during such illness or absence shall have all the powers of a Revising Officer, and if he is not a Judge of any court his decision shall be subject to appeal as provided in the Act hereby amended.

Qualification and powers of such deputy.

(*f*) As pointed out in note (*a*) p. 168 of the original work, the Revising Officer could not delegate this power of adjournment to his clerk ; and an irregular adjournment would vitiate the proceedings of the Revision Court. See note (*d*) p. 159 of the original work. The sessions of the Peace cannot be adjourned by the crier, without the presence of the justices : *Rex* v. *Middlesex*, 5 B. & Ad. 1113.

(*g*) This varies the rule of law, that a Judicial Officer cannot appoint a deputy or delegate his judicial functions to another as pointed out in note (*a*) p. 168 of the original work. A person appointed to some function or office to which peculiar personal skill is essential cannot delegate his functions or office to another : *St. Margaret* v. *Thompson*, L. R. 6 C. P. 445.

(*h*) This approval must be obtained before such Deputy Revising Officer can execute any of the duties of his office.

(*i*) The qualifications of a Revising Officer are set out in s. 14 of the original Act. And as to the Deputy taking the oath of office prescribed for Revising Officers, it may be noted that the original Act (s. 13) requires the Revising Officer "before entering upon his duties," to take an oath of office before any Judge of a Superior Court of Record. By the *Interpretation Act* 31 Vic. c. 1, s. 7 subs. 28 it is declared that "words *directing* or empowering

Polling district not to be subdivided in case specified.

18. In the present year, one thousand eight hundred and eighty-six, it shall not be necessary, in any case in which the preliminary list of voters has been made for a polling district constituted under the laws in force at the time of the passing of the said Act, (*j*) and does not contain the names of more than three hundred voters, that such polling district should be divided as provided by section twenty-one of the said Act; and in every such case the final revision shall be made upon such preliminary list, and it shall not be necessary that such list shall be printed and published as provided by section twenty-four of the said Act, (*k*) but the notice of the final revision required by the last cited section, and section

---

a public officer or functionary *to do any act* or thing, or otherwise applying to him by his name of office, shall include his successors in such office, and his or their lawful *deputy.*" A deputy judge has no authority to deliver judgment after the expiration of the period for which he was appointed, or after the death of the judge who appointed him : *Hoey v. Macfarlane,* 4 C. B. N. S. 71.

(*j*) "The laws in force at the time of the passing of the said Act," under which polling districts were constituted, were the provisions in s. 11 of the Dominion Elections Act, 1874, by which the Returning Officer for an election was directed to recognize the subdivisions into polling districts made by the Legislature or by the local authorities under the legislation of the Province, if made ; and if not so made, then to divide the Electoral District into polling divisions for the purposes of such election.

(*k*) The effect of this is to repeal so much of the original Act as required (1) the printing of the voters' list after the preliminary revision ; (2) the posting of copies of such list in three conspicuous public places in each of the polling districts ; and (3) the delivery of copies to persons applying for the same and upon payment of certain fees. It is not necessary to consider whether the other provisions of that section—requiring the delivery of such lists to the public officers and persons named—are or are not essential to the

twenty-five of the said Act may be posted up and published at any time after the passing of this Act. (*l.*)

19. The list of voters prepared under the said Act in the present year, one thousand eight hundred and eighty-six, shall when finally revised, be valid and shall avail for the purposes of the said Act, notwithstanding that any form thereby prescribed is departed from, or that anything done is not done within the time or in the manner prescribed thereby, (*m*) or that the territorial limits assigned to the Revising Officers in the district of Algoma were altered or extended subsequently to their having taken the oath of office : (*n*)

Certain lists of 1886 to be valid.

---

due publication of such lists, as the above section is temporary in its operation.

(*l*) By s. 26 of the original Act this notice of the final revision must be published by "one insertion in a newspaper ;" but though the day to be named in the notice "shall not be less than five weeks after the publication by posting up of the lists," the date of the publication of the notice is left to the discretion of the Revising Officer.

(*m*) This provision is in harmony with the rules for the construction of such directions in a statute referred to in notes (*h*) p. 99, (*m*) p. 119, (*p*) p. 135, and elsewhere in the original work. Where certain voters had sent in their claims in good time, but the officer did not publish their names on the list of voters until after the statutory time,—the statute providing that "a disregard of any form or instruction shall not of itself invalidate any list, notice, or other thing :" *Held* that as the consequences of allowing an objection to the list would be to give the registering officer the power of disfranchising persons entitled to the franchise who had done all they could to obtain it, such neglect did not invalidate the lists : *Wells* v. *Stanforth*, 10 Q. B. D. 244. But declarations sent to the Revising Barrister after the statutory time cannot be acted upon : *Daking* v. *Fraser*, 16 Q. B. D. 252.

(*n*) The territorial limits of the Electoral District of Algoma were defined by the B. N. A. Act, sec. 40, and in No. 44 in the first schedule, as " the Pro-

No action
shall lie
against
revising
officers for
Algoma.

2. No action or proceeding shall lie or be maintained against the Revising Officers in the said district of Algoma, for any penalty or penalties by reason of their acting as such revising officers after the limits assigned to them had been changed and new commissions had been issued to them without taking their oaths of office anew.

Oath of
qualification
of a voter at
elections.

20. The oath of qualification to be administered to a voter under the provisions of the section substituted by section six (o) of the Act forty-first Victoria, chapter six, for section forty-three of "*The Dominion Elections Act*, 1874," shall be in the form B or in one of the forms C, D, E, F or G, in the schedule to this Act, as the circumstances of the case require. (p)

---

visional Judicial District of Algoma;" and by 45 Vic. ch. 3, (D.) which provides that "the settlements westward of the Provisional District of Thunder Bay and eastward of the Electoral Districts of Manitoba, shall pending the adjustment of the Boundaries, be and the same are hereby made part of the Electoral District of Algoma." The territory known as "Thunder Bay," was constituted a Territorial District by the proclamation of the Lieutenant-Governor of Ontario, dated 1st June, 1871, pursuant to the Act 34 Vic. ch. 4, (O). It formed the chief portion of the "Disputed Territory" between the Dominion and Ontario, and was found to be a part of Ontario by the award of the arbitrators made on the 3rd August, 1878. It was subsequently consti-tuted a Judicial District by the Act 47 Vic. ch 14 (O); and on the 22nd July, 1884, the boundaries described in the award of the 3rd August, 1878 were declared by the Judicial Committee of the Imperial Privy Council to be the true boun-daries of Ontario, as between that Province and the Province of Manitoba.

(o) This is a mistake. The section intended is sec. 5 of the Act of 1878, and not sec. 6 ; see 41 Vic. ch. 6, (D.)

(p) By the Registration Act, 6 Vic. c. 18 s. 81, (Imp.) it is provided that at elections for the Imperial House of Commons no inquiry as to the right of a person to vote, is allowed, except by two questions, (1) "Are you the same person whose name appears as A. B. on the register of voters now in force for the county," &c ? and (2), "Have you already voted here or elsewhere at this election for the county," &c ? And, if required on behalf of any candi-date, the voter must take an oath to the same effect.

SCHEDULE.

FORM A.
LIST OF VOTERS

For the year commencing 1st June, 18 , for the Polling District No. of the (*Municipality* 6 of, or the City or Town, or as the case may be) of) in the Electoral District of

LIST OF POST OFFICES WITH THEIR REFERENCE NUMBERS.

1. Campbelltown.	4. Iona.	7. Port Talbot.
2. Cowal.	5. Iona Station.	8. Tyrconnel.
3. Dutton.	6. Largie.	9. Wallacetown.

POLLING DISTRCT No. .

Comprising all the Lots and Parts of Lots in the following territory : Bounded on or towards the South by , and on the East by , on the North by , on the West by , (*or as the case may be.*)

Consecutive Number.	Name in Full. — (*Surname first.*)	Occupation.	Post Office Address.	Nature and Title of Qualification.	Concession, Street and No. of Lot, or other sufficient description of property; and residence if qualified on income, or as son of owner or farmer's son, with name of owner or farmer in the case of owner's or farmer's sons.
1	Atkinson, Alfred ..	Carpenter ..	9	Son of owner......	Lot 21, con. 3, John Atkinson.
2	Adams, Wm. Henry	Farmer	8	Owner.........	N. W. pt. lot 28, con. 6.
3	Asseltine, Pierre ..	Stonemason..	1	Tenant	Pt. 20, broken front, Rideau.
4	Benjamin, Ernest..	Bricklayer ..	7	Income	667 Wellington street, W.
5	Bisonnette, Paul....	Fisherman ..	4	Fisherman and owner.	Pt. 34, Range No. 10.
6	Brennan, Edward ..	Plasterer	2	Income	18 Broad street.
7	Campion, Francis..	Farmer	3	Farmer's son..	Lot 31, con. 4, Peter Campion.
8	Cooper, Charles ...	Printer	5	Tenant	Pt. 10, East George street.
9	Clegge, William ..	Painter	6	Occupant	Lot 14, Elgin street.

Dated   188

A. B.,
Revising Officer for the electoral district (or part of the electoral district of

FORM B.

Form of Oath of Qualification of a person whose name is registered as a voter on the list of voters otherwise than as a farmer's son or as the son of the owner of other real property.

I, (A.B.) solemnly swear (*or if he is one of the persons permitted by law to affirm in civil cases,* solemnly affirm),—

1. That I am the person named, or purporting to be named, by the name of   (*and if there are more persons than one of the same name on the said list, inserting also his addition or occupation*) on the list of voters for polling district No.   in the electoral district (*or municipality*) of

2. That I am a British subject (by birth *or* naturalization, *as the case may be*) and that I am of the full age of twenty-one years :

3. That I have not voted before at this election, either at this or any other polling place :

4. That I have not received anything, nor has anything been promised me, directly or indirectly, either to induce me to vote at this election, or for loss of time, travelling expenses, hire of team, or for any other service connected therewith :

5. That I have not, directly or indirectly, paid or promised anything to any person either to induce him to vote or to refrain from voting at this election. So help me God.

FORM C.

Form of Oath of Qualification of a person whose name is registered as a voter on the list of voters, as being a farmer's son not claiming the benefit of the provisions as to occasional absence as a mariner, fisherman or student.

I, (A.B.), solemnly swear (*or if he is one of the persons permitted by law to affirm in civil cases,* solemnly affirm),—

1. That I am the person named, or purporting to be named, by the name of   (*and if there are more persons than one of the same name on the said list, inserting also his addition or occupation*) on the list of voters for polling district No.   in the electoral district (*or municipality*) of

2. That I am a British subject (by birth *or* naturalization, *as the case may be*) and that I am of the full age of twenty-one years :

3. That I have not voted before at this election, either at this or any other polling place :

4. That I have not received anything, nor has anything been promised me, directly or indirectly, either to induce me to vote at this election, or for loss of time, travelling expenses, hire of team or for any other service connected therewith :

5. That I have not, directly or indirectly, paid or promised anything to any person, either to induce him to vote or to refrain from voting at this election :

6. That I am resident with my father (*or if his father is dead*, with my mother) within this electoral district, and that I have not been absent from such residence more than six months since I was placed on the list of voters· So help me God.

FORM D.

Form of Oath of Qualification of a person whose name is registered as a voter on the list of voters as being the son of the owner of real property, other than a farm, not claiming the benefit of the provision as to occasional absence as a mariner, fisherman, or student.

I, (A.B.), solemnly swear (*or if he is one of the persons permitted by law to affirm in civil cases*, solemnly affirm),—

1. That I am the person named, or purporting to be named, by the name of   (*and if there are more persons than one of the same name on the said list, inserting also his addition or occupation*) on the list of voters for polling district No.   in the electoral district (*or municipality*) of

2. That I am a British subject (by birth *or* naturalization, *as the case may be*) and that 1 am of the full age of twenty-one years :

3. That I have not voted before at this election, either at this or any other polling place :

4. That I have not received anything nor has anything been promised me, directly or indirectly, either to induce me to vote at this election or for loss of time, travelling expenses, hire of team, or for any other service connected therewith :

5. That I have not, directly or indirectly, paid or promised anything to any person, either to induce him to vote or to refrain from voting at this election :

6. That I am resident with my father (or *if his father is dead*, with my mother) within this electoral district, and that I have not been absent from such residence more than six months since I was placed on the list of voters. So help me God.

FORM E.

Form of Oath of Qualification of a person whose name is registered as a voter on the list of voters as a farmer's son and claiming the benefit of the provision as to occasional absence as a mariner, fisherman, or student.

I, (A. B.), solemnly swear (or *if he is one of the persons permitted by law to affirm in civil cases*, solemnly affirm),—

1. That I am the person named or purporting to be named, by the name of   (*and if there are more persons than one of the same name on the said list, inserting also his addition or occupation*) on the list of voters for polling district No.   in the electoral district (*or municipality*) of   :

2. That I am a British subject (by birth *or naturalization, as the case may be*) and that I am of the full age of twenty-one years :

3. That I have not voted before at this election, either at this or any other polling place :

4. That I have not received anything nor has anything been promised me, directly or indirectly, either to induce me to vote at this election or for loss of time, travelling expenses, hire of team or for any other service connected therewith :

5. That I have not directly or indirectly, paid or promised anything to any person either to induce him to vote or to refrain from voting at this election :

6. That I am resident with my father (or *if his father is dead*, with my mother) within this electoral district. That I am a mariner (or a fisherman *or a student in an institution of learning in Canada, as the case may be*), and that I have not been absent from such residence for more than six months since I was placed on said list of voters, except in the exercise of my occupation as such mariner, (fisherman, *or student, as the case may be*). So help me God.

FORM F.

*Form of Oath of Qualification of a person whose name is registered as a voter·
on the list of voters as the son of an owner of real property other than a.
farm and claiming the benefit of the provision as to occasional absence, as a
mariner, fisherman, or student.*

I, (A. B.), solemnly swear (*or if he is one of the persons permitted by law to·
affirm in civil cases,* solemnly affirm),—

1. That I am the person named, or purporting to be named, by the name
of
(*and if there are more persons than one of the same name on the said list inserting also his addition or occupation*) on the list of voters for polling district.
No.   in the Electoral District (*or municipality*) of

2. That I am a British subject (by birth *or* naturalization, *as the case may·
be*) and that I am of the full age of twenty-one years :

3. That I have not voted before at this election, either at this or at any
other polling place.

4. That I have not received anything nor has anything been promised me,.
directly or indirectly, either to induce me to vote at this election or for loss.
of time, travelling expenses, hire of team or for any other service connected
therewith :

5. That I have not, directly or indirectly, paid or promised anything to·
any person either to induce him to vote or to refrain from voting at this.
election :

6. That I am a resident with my father (*or if his father is dead,* with my
mother) within this Electoral District. That I am a mariner (*or* fisherman,
or a student in an institution of learning in Canada, *as the case may be*) and
that I have not been absent from such residence for more than six months.
since I was placed on the said list of voters except in the exercise of my
occupation as a mariner (*or* fisherman *or* student, *as the case may be*). So
help me God.

FORM G.

*Form of oath of qualification of a person who has been excluded from the list of·
voters, and which exclusion appears by the list of voters to be the subject of
an undecided appeal.*

I, (A. B.), solemnly swear (*or if he be one of the persons permitted by law to·
affirm in civil cases,* solemnly affirm),—

1. That I (*stating residence, post office address and addition or occupation*) duly applied before the Revising Officer for the Electoral District of (*or portion of an Electoral District, as the case may be, in which the polling district where such person applies for a ballot paper is situated*) to have my name registered on the list of voters for this polling district (*or in the case of the first lists made for such Electoral District or portion of an Electoral District* on the list or one of the lists of voters for such Electoral District, or portion of an Electoral District,) under the provisions of "The Electoral Franchise Act:"

2. That my application to have my name so registered was refused; that I have duly appealed from such decision of the said Revising Officer, pursuant to the provisions of the said Act:

3. That I am a British subject (by birth *or* naturalization *as the case may be*) and that I am of the full age of twenty-one years:

4. That I have not voted before at this election, either at this or any other polling place:

5. That I have not received anything nor has anything been promised me, directly or indirectly, either to induce me to vote at this election or for loss of time, travelling expenses, hire of team or for any other service connected therewith:

6. That I have not directly or indirectly, paid or promised anything to any person either to induce him to vote or to refrain from voting at this election:

7. (*Also if the claim of such person to be entitled to be registered on the list of voters and to vote is as a farmer's son or as the son of an owner of real property other than a farmer, and if the subject of such appeal is the exclusion of his name from such list as such son*) That I am resident with my father (or *if his father is dead*, with my mother) within this Electoral District. *If the person is a mariner, fisherman or student, claiming the benefit of the provision as to occasional absence add:* "that I am a mariner (*or* fisherman or student at an institution of learning in Canada, *as the case may be*) and that I have not been absent from such residence more than six months since my said application to be placed on the list of voters. So help me God.

INDEX.

EVIDENCE, 10 ; Assessment Rolls, *prima facie*, 9, 13, 32.

" FARM," definition of, 9.

" FARMERS' SONS," definition of amended, 8 ; qualification of, 15, 18 ; include tenant-farmers' Sons, 8 ; how far such are included, 8, 9, 15, 19.

" FATHER," definition of amended, 8.

FATHER-IN-LAW included in " father," 8.

FINAL REVISION of voters' lists : when to be completed, 26 ; time for altered, 31, 36.

FINE for non-attendance on Revision Court, 35.

FISHERMEN, franchise extended to cities and towns, 22 ; qualification amended, 22 ; absence as, 26.

FORM of voters' lists amended, 36, 41 ; departure from not to be invalidate lists, 39.

FRANCHISE, table of qualifications for, 4 ; a trust in those qualified, 29 ; husband the representative of wife in, 7.

FREE AND COMMON SOCCAGE, 7.

FREEHOLD ESTATE, 6.

FULL AGE, 10.

GRANDFATHER included in " father," 8.

GRANDMOTHER included in " mother," 8.

GRANDSON included in " son," 9.

HUSBAND, his right to qualify for his wife's property, 6 ; when representative of his wife in voting, 7 ; his right of possession of his wife's property, 8, 14.

HEARING of appeal in absence of complainant, 29.

INCOME VOTER, amendment as to residences, 14, 15 ; qualification of, 14.

INFANTS, names of, should be struck off the list, 10.

INFORMATION, Revising Officer's proceedings on, 9, 31.

7

INSPECTION of documents relating to voters' lists, a common law right, 27.

INTERPRETATION of terms : "Owner," 6 ; "Occupant," 8 ; "Father," 8 ; "Mother," 8 ; "Son," 9 ; "Farmers' Son," 8 ; "Son of Owner," 9 ; "Actual Value," 9 ; "Value," 9.

JUDGE-MADE-LAW, Austin's remarks on, 18.
JURISDICTION of Revision Court, 27.

LEGAL INCAPACITY TO VOTE, persons subject to should be struck off list, 10.
LICENSE OF OCCUPATION, amendment respecting, 13.
LIST OF VOTERS for 1886 made valid, 38, 39.

MANDAMUS, writ of, lies to enforce inspection of documents, 28.
MARRIED WOMEN'S PROPERTY ACTS, 7.
MINORS, should be struck off the Lists, 10.
MISDESCRIPTION, power to amend, 29.
MISTAKES in Voters' List, power to amend, 30.
"MOTHER" definition of, 8 ; when owner of farm, 17 , when tenant of farm, 17.
MOTHER-IN-LAW, included in "mother," 8.

NOTICES, may be written or printed, 33 ; service of, 34 ; inspection of, 27.
NON-ATTENDANCE at Revision Court, substitute in case of, 29 ; punishment for such non-attendance, 34,35.

OATHS for voters at the poll, 6, 42-46.
OBJECTOR, bound to attend Revision Court, 33 ; substitute on non-attendance, 29.
"OCCUPANT," amended definition of, 8; qualification of, 13 ; when wife occupant, 8, 14.
OCCUPATION, qualifying period of, 11, 13, 14, 24.
"OWNER," definition of, 6 ; qualification of, 11 ; when wife proprietor, 6.
OWNERS' Sons franchise, 19.

www.ingramcontent.com/pod-product-compliance
Lightning Source LLC
Chambersburg PA
CBHW021643270326
41931CB00008B/1145